To Dr. Roger Goodwin as a token of appreciation of his friendliness and the spiritual depth of his sermons in the historical Baptist in Grandview; with sincerest respect and brotherhood,

Carl B. Rayburn.

TUS-KEE-MAH
OF THE DESERT

TUS-KEE-MAH OF THE DESERT

and other poems

by

Carl Bryan Rayburn

VANTAGE PRESS
New York   Washington   Atlanta   Hollywood

FIRST EDITION

All rights reserved, including the right of
reproduction in whole or in part in any form.

Copyright © 1979 by Carl Bryan Rayburn

Published by Vantage Press, Inc.
516 West 34th Street, New York, New York 10001

Manufactured in the United States of America
Standard Book Number 533-03625-9

Library of Congress Catalog Card No.: 78-51780

DEDICATION

To my wife Pansie, our son, William Candler, and our daughters, Frances Lucile, Mary Louise, and Helen Ruth, in grateful recognition of those sacred family bonds which, deepened by hallowed memories, remain a source of joy and inspiration through the years.

CONTENTS

Introduction, by Chief Standing Bear

Tus-Kee-Mah of the Desert	1
Oo-Loo-Te-Ka's Death Song	8
Grey Wolf of the Hassayampa	11
Chief Joseph's Address to His Warriors	14
Ode to the Evening Star	19
Mercury on His Lyre	21
The Rescue of the Enemy	24
Winds of Winter	29
A Parting Hymn	30
Name No More the Day We Met	31
I Waited for You	32
Memories in Winter	33
The Spring at the End of the Trail	34
A Father Remembers	36
Asleep on the Hill	37
A Song of the Years	38
Now and Eternity	39
The Last Banquet	40
For Old Times' Sake	42
Sing Us a Song	43
A Pioneer to His Wife	44
A Long Hunter's Song	45
The Elf and the Fairy	46
The Capture of Tim Knott	47
The Last Family Reunion	50
To My Children	51
The Farewell	52
To One in Heaven	53
The Dreamer	54

The Stage of Life	55
On the Death of a Friend	56
To a Cherokee Hunter	57
Ghosts at Wounded Knee	58
To a Philosopher	59
Inscribed to Eric James Rollins	60
To Colonel Elijah C. Kirtley, Scholar and Humanitarian	61
In Memory of Mrs. Margaret Mitchell	62
In Memory of Mrs. Mary Gossett	63
On the Death of Sir Winston Churchill	64
On the Cause of Peace	65
On Mozart's *Magic Flute*	66
Liladore	67
Rose of the South	68
On Love in Youth	69
If You No Longer Care	70
A Husband's Apology	71
Egypt	72
On Tacitus	73
To William Candler Rayburn	74
On Abraham Lincoln's Birthplace	75
On the Reclamation of Art	76

INTRODUCTION

In the pages of this volume—*TUS-KEE-MAH OF THE DESERT And Other Poems*—the writer has shared with us his high spirit of life appreciation. In stanzaic form he has embodied gems of philosophical thought, while in lengthy narrative form he has placed in poetic garb factual matter concerning the Indian.

These rugged verses ring with satisfying authenticity. They sing unpretentiously of an unpretentious life—rich and brimming with sympathy.

Here is a white man who understands universality and the sacredness of nature as the Indian understood it; who has glimpsed the Red Man's world where "the waters flowed with gladness" and in which world the Indian once partook of the strength of Wakan Tanka.

This contact has touched the writer, and his memory of it is vivid; for he writes,

>Be not surprised if the broken measure
>Is plain at times and the rhythm rough;
>But if you can see, you will find the treasure
>Of a friendship true, and that is enough.

In solitude with Tus-kee-mah the writer found the enchantment that the Indian found in the desert, mesa, and canyon walls. In these years he learned to love the land "where the cactus stand guard of the desert's treasured lore" and to find the "cosmic peace of the ages."

In "Chief Joseph's Address" we find a spirit touched with fine understanding of the Indian—an appreciation of his disappointment and despair in his relations with the white man. The author frankly sets forth the injustice of the white man, his needless cruelty, "dark deeds" on which the eyes of civilization looked with strong approval. And, too, he heard the bitter, futile outcry of the Red Man. In this sense the poem is masterly.

Much of a scientific nature has been written about the native people of America but scientific treatises reach only a limited public. In recent years, however, fine novelistic works have had the effect of widening and humanizing public concern in the Indian.

But there is still room for poetic treatment of Indian history and legendry; for the appeal of poetry reached the heart of the world. A vast store of Indian history awaits narration by the white poet who has caught the spirit of the soil. In the artistic richness of poetry a wealth of indigenous lore and history might not only find wide appeal but be preserved for posterity.

This author has kindled my keen appreciation for his earnestness, courage, and vivid understanding. May his volume go forth to do likewise for other readers.

CHIEF STANDING BEAR
Huntington Park, California

TUS-KEE-MAH
OF THE DESERT

TUS-KEE-MAH OF THE DESERT

As Told by an Old Prospector

This is a chant, not an armchair story,
    Of life in the West when the days were hard;
Of the Desert Land in its primal glory
    When the soul of a man was his own reward.
Be not surprised if the broken measure
    Is plain at times and the rhythm rough;
But if you can see, you will find the treasure
    Of a friendship true, and that is enough.

Tus-kee-mah and I, like two loyal brothers,
    Wandered afar, ere the trails were old,
Over that desolate region where others
    Hunted and fought and died for the gold.
But nothing our comradeship could sever,
    Though heat or starvation haunted the way;
And neither deserted the other, whatever
    Blighted the night or threatened the day.

From Alkali Lake to the Santa Rita
    From Pecos stream to the Joaquin plains,
Beyond the springs of the Chil-chi-vita
    We led our burros and nursed our pains:
Full twenty long years of toil and danger
    We wandered in canyon and cactus land;—
But if you are not a prospector or ranger,
    Never on earth will you understand.

Well I remember that morning in summer
> When first I met him—at Antelope Spring:
The Desert's breath was so hot that no hummer
> Nor hawk nor eagle stirred on the wing;
Slowly he drank where the stream was narrow,
> Unaware that a stranger watched out of sight;
No weapon he bore, not even an arrow,
> And weak he appeared as if from long flight.

Naw-wauch[1] I called him, gave him some *tee-wah*[2],
> Learned he had fled from Awps for three suns;
Then, seeing the grateful eyes of Tus-kee-mah,
> I handed him one of my two black guns.
Arising, he made the sign of Taw-haw-no[3]
> Under the shade of the wild *suk-koy;*
Then we, both repeating the ancient *se-gaw-no,*[4]
> Shook hands in the sight of the good *Ee-e-toy.*[5]

He was a Papago, braver than lucky,
> Swift on the trail as a *pahn koor-lee,*[6]
And I was a paleface, strayed from Kentucky,
> Youthful, hardened, and as brown as he.
Together we struck for the steep Colorado,
> Crossed it, and made for the first gold field,
Determined to find, on the trail of Coronado,
> The mines where Spain once planted her shield.

For months, at first, with the hard-rock miners,
> We sifted and dug near old Vulture Camp,
Then crossed the trail of the Forty-niners,
> Forever dreaming of a profitable tramp:
But always the strike just ahead was better
> Or worse than the ones we had made before;

Notes: [1]Naw-wauch, friend. [2]Tee-wah, moccasins. [3]Taw-haw-no, the desert.
[4]Se-gaw-no, covenant or pledge. [5]Ee-e-toy, the Great Spirit.
[6]Pahn koor-lee, a large wolf.

Fortune was waiting, but never we met her
    By the mountainside or the river shore.

In those hazardous years Arizona was wilder
    Than your sightseeing tourists can dream,
But civilization has molded her milder
    Than the placid wave of her slowest stream;
Where the Pullman speeds, once the prairie schooner
    Halted and screaked through the crawling sand,
And the fisherman cooks on his oil-stove sooner
    Than old-timers could gather the brush at hand.

Where we slept in mesquite and creosote branches,
    With irrigated crops the landscape now thrives,
And adventurous tourists ride over dude ranches,
    Tanning their faces for once in their lives;
Where thirsty men sought the haunts of the beaver
    Or fell in the heat with a prayer or a curse,
Electrical breezes cool the brow of fever,
    And illness is attended by doctor and nurse.

Far up in the loneliest primitive places,
    Camping on plateaus of the eagle and owl,
Tus-kee-mah and I watched the cunning faces
    Of creatures that ventured at dusk to prowl;
And sometimes at night, by the crest of the canyon,
    As springtime approached from the valley below,
We heard the wild cougar call its companion,
    Or a lone wolf howl on a summit of snow.

On many an eve, when the moon's full magic
    Shaded the wooded slopes of the range,
My comrade chanted old tribal legends,
    Lofty traditions, and narratives strange

In all their wild beauty, till I learned why Huwuhleh[7]
  Forces slow Choovahk[8] across the wild sky;
Why Juhfaw[9] and Choomahmike[10] live in the desert,
  And when Nahkukmuhlee[11] first became shy.

On a few occasions, by the cliff's ample cave
  That yielded no sign of the nuggets we sought,
I told him of cities that mastered the wave
  Of the Nile before Cyrus in Babylon fought;
Or, recalling the tales in a Grecian book,
  Repeated the plays by old Sophocles,
Watched Troy's walls which the conflict shook,
  Or pondered the wisdom of Socrates.

There in that loneliest land of the lizard,
  Rattlesnake, gopher, and coyote long,
Historic in fossils, erosion, and blizzard,
  Undiscovered by art and classical song,
We felt the deep cosmic peace of the ages
  Transcending all hope, all sorrow, all mirth,
Profounder by far than the wisdom of sages,
  Far older by aeons than mankind's birth.

And I knew, as we bowed in the mystic presence
  Of the God whose love in the sunset shone,
In Tus-kee-mah's heart was the very essence
  Of the worship the blessed Christ might own:
In the brotherly bonds of mortal existence
  The life of my friend was akin to mine,
And both were stirred by the deep insistence
  Of longings that look to that Power divine.

So through the years, as we constantly drifted
  From desert to plain, from mesa to town,
For each other the load of life we lifted,
  Whether our fortunes were up or down.

Notes: 7. Huwuhleh, the wind. 8. Choo-vahk, a cloud. 9. Juhfaw, the gopher. 10. Choo-mah-mike, the horned toad. 11. Nahkukmuhlee, the bat.

Never a word of harshness was spoken,
    No jibe unless softened by humor's breath;
Never the bond of our fellowship broken
    To the solemn day of Tus-kee-mah's death.

In the lawless years, when Tombstone counted
    Its victims inducted under the sod,
And the two-gun men and the gamblers mounted
    In favor with others by threat or nod,
Two peaceable comrades, pausing to linger
    Where sharkies played for the last gold grain,
Listened a while to the dance hall singer
    And ate at half-civilized tables again.

We kept to ourselves—for a very good reason,
    Kept our opinions under our hat;
For some in that camp were the soul of treason,
    And some were as low as a kangaroo rat.
But a few were trustworthy, as Tennessee Rider,
    One of the quickest ever forced to a draw,
Who, wounding both arms of bad Klondike Snyder,
    Once taunted the town for its lack of law.

And once in Yosemite a reckless man made
    A spiteful attempt on a parson's life:
He drew on the sand a coffin and spade,
    Then suddenly brandished a murderous knife;
But the minister struck like a lightning bolt,
    The weapon went flying over the crowd,
And the two went down with a sudden jolt,
    Stirring the dust to a rolling cloud.

When the scuffle ended, the preacher arose,
    Helped the other to his tottering feet,
Shook him almost out of his clothes,
    And made him the Ten Commandments repeat;

Then on the astonished street they knelt
    As the minister prayed for the souls of both,
While some gunmen nervously fingered a belt,
    And some exploded with wondering oath.

From the Amargosa once I tried to follow
    A mountain lion through the ranges far,
Till, lost in the distance of peak and hollow,
    I sought direction by the evening star:
Thirst became torture, and each step was haunted
    By the heat as I desperately staggered on;
The menacing mesas their enmity flaunted,
    And I knew, as I fell, that the desert had won.

Helpless I lay when Tus-kee-mah found me,
    Guided by vultures that circled on high;
And death, whose arms already were round me,
    Relinquished his hold but lingered nigh:
O'er many a mile a courageous shoulder
    Bore me across the formidable sands
To the beckoning shade of old Piute Boulder,
    Most blessed spot of the desert lands.

Life in those years became an adventure
    That yielded its nobler meaning at last,
Naught but low motive deserving of censure,
    Nothing but manhood surviving the past;—
Misfortunes came, though we never did choose them,
    We met them with shields of willingness drawn;
And some riches we gained, never to lose them,
    Things of the soul—not the world's cheap pawn.

Twenty swift years! Then we stopped on our way
    At Antelope Spring in search of a deer.
But sickness overtook Tus-kee-mah that day,
    And soon we knew his departure was near:
On the next day at dusk, at the very spot
    Where our friendship here on earth began,

We watched death's approach but mentioned not
    The unutterable thoughts that filled each man.

Feebly he made the sign of Taw-haw-no
    In the grieving shade of the wild *suk-koy*,
Slowly I chanted the ancient *se-gaw-no*,
    And we lifted our hands in pledge to *Ee-e-toy*,
As we had years ago. One solemn finger
    He raised in salute to the years of the past,
Where his ebbing memory seemed to linger
    Till he yielded his spirit at last.

The name of my comrade my soul shall cherish,
    And memories that hallow the sunset sky,
Till the glory of dawn on the desert perish,
    Till the spotted eagle forget to fly:
Pondering here the whence and the whither
    Of the spirit, I know Tus-kee-mah has found
The other Desert where no flowers wither
    And no thirst nor hunger inhabit the ground.

OO-LOO-TE-KA'S DEATH SONG

Where lordly cottonwoods looked down
  On silent summer plains serene,
And watched above the banks of brown
  The Arkansas that flowed between,
    Outside his spacious wigwam lay
    Chief Oo-loo-te-ka, worn and gray.

Upon the knoll within the wood,
  His people waiting for the end,
The aged warrior rose and stood,
  As day and dusk began to blend,
    And chanted forth this song ere death
    Claimed for her own his feeble breath:—

"Farewell, my children; Day is o'er,
  And Oo-loo-te-ka hears the sound
Of voices on another shore
  That call him to the Hunting Ground;
    But ere he crosses, he would tell
    What sorrows with his people dwell.

"The Cherokees, in years gone by,
  Dwelt in the forest of the brave,
Where eagles swept the mountain sky
  And deer fed by the cliff and cave:
From Nan-ta-ha they held the land
To wild Kentucky's bloody strand.

"They were a nation proud and bold,
  And strong alike in peace and war;
Brave were those warrior chiefs of old
  That drove the hostile tribesmen far,—
    They loved the right and banished wrong,
    No tribe so valiant, none so strong.

"In time, alas! the paleface came
  Upon our lands with axe and gun,
Wrote each new treaty in his name,
  But broke it ere the morning sun;
    And Cherokees their honor proved,—
    They left the land and westward moved!

"Where still the Hiawassee bounds
  Its rapid way through leaping foam,
There Oo-loo-te-ka loved the sounds
  Of nature round his island home,
    Till in the years that music grew
    The dearest song the highlands knew.

"But careless hands had signed away
  Our ancient homes in Tennessee
For barren knobs and plains that lay
  Where red men might again be free;
    And Oo-loo-te-ka led his band
    Out to the dreaded Darkening Land.

"Hills of my birth! the eagles swoop
  No longer round your rugged crags!
Their mourning heads the forests droop
  Where fled of old the hunted stags!
    You hear no Indian voice at last
    Except an echo of the past!

"Decay now claims that lonely isle
  Where games and laughter once abode;

O'er it Yo-he-wah ceased to smile,
　　Dim are the paths my people strode:
　　　　Of all the sounds the vales have known
　　　　They hear how faint the chants have grown.

"But now the bow and spear shall yield
　　Their place to busy hoe and plow:
Fierce Tah-lhon-tusky's fearless shield
　　Are by the tribes forgotten now;
　　　　The Cherokee, Choctaw, and Creek
　　　　Shall now one language learn to speak.

"And here the Cherokees shall find
　　A home where Ta-ka-ta found rest,
And to their nation peace shall bind
　　The tribes that wander farther west:
　　　　Once more the Cherokees shall claim
　　　　The glory of their ancient name.

"Farewell, my children. Night has come;
　　The dark winds whisper o'er the plain.
Bid yonder shaman now be dumb;
　　For Oo-loo-te-ka hears again
　　　　The sound, as on another shore,
　　　　Of voices louder than before."

GREY WOLF OF THE HASSAYAMPA

He was known from Pelonchillo
    To Death Valley's haunted sands
As Grey Wolf of Hassayampa,—
    Phantom of the cactus lands:
Silent, grim, alert, and stealthy,
    He was neither friend nor foe
To the camps in that wild region
    Where he wandered to and fro.

Rumor told a hundred stories
    Of this figure tall and strange,
Wondered at his constant prowess
    On the mesa, cliff, and range;
And prospectors still repeated
    How dark slander used a bribe
That had made the lonely Indian
    Aw-o-tahm, without a tribe.

Once I saw him on the desert
    Near old Winnemucca bleak:
Like a ghost he stole upon us
    From that solitary peak;
Scarce a second glance he gave me,
    But his eyes were keen and swift
As he watched the two Apaches
    Lead our burros past the drift.

East and west of Vegas Valley,
    Ere the foothills saw a town,
In the camps for days he lingered,
    Never heeding smile or frown;
But whene'er an Indian entered,
    Something in the Grey Wolf's face
Made him hurry from the presence
    Of the outcast of his race.

From the Humboldt to the border,
    Over lands the eagle fears,
Long he searched, as on a mission,
    With the patience of the years:
Plain, sierra, foothill, canyon,
    Mesa, range, and lava bed
Came to know his noiseless footstep
    As they did the coyote's tread.

Many a summer, many a winter,
    Grey Wolf made his stark abode
With the quick pink-throated lizard,
    Prairie dog, and horned toad;
Oft he drank the cactus syrup,
    Trapped for food the birds at dawn,
Dried the venison by the cascade
    Where the herd at dusk was drawn.

Then one day in drowsy Yucca,
    When the Wash beyond was deep,
Grey Wolf, watching in the barroom,
    Spied a Navajo asleep.
Drawing near, he saw the features
    Of a foe that memory knew,
And he lightly touched the other
    As his hunting knife he drew.

Forty feet away the weapon
    Pierced a post across the room,
And the Navajo stared helpless
    Like a man who reads his doom.
But Grey Wolf, his hand uplifted
    In the sign of brotherhood,
Speaking words of strange assurance,
    Calm before the other stood.

Calm and solemn and majestic,
    In that hour he held his prey
With the matchless strength of mercy
    Ere he slowly turned away
From the man whose crime dark slander
    Laid on Grey Wolf through a bribe,—
Turned his face toward Hassayampa,
    Aw-o-tahm, without a tribe.

CHIEF JOSEPH'S ADDRESS TO HIS WARRIORS

On Surrendering to General Nelson A. Miles

My brother warriors, heavy is the voice
Of Hin-mah-too-yah-lat-kekt, last free chief
Who led, till yesterday, the Chute-pa-lu
Against greed's bloody conquest:—may our hearts,
These months undaunted in unequal strife,
Still find some comfort in the ancient bonds
Of tribal faith, which strong men cherish most
In famine and defeat. As warriors who
Have ceased from hopeless struggle only that
Our wives and children might not fall beneath
The shadow, let us backward turn our eyes
Unto the peaceful years when sun and stars
Looked gently on our fathers' fair abode;
For it may be that, as we name the wrongs
Inflicted without cause upon the homes
Which once were ours, the face of Wakan Tanka
Again shall turn toward our people in
Their hungry suffering, and He may hear
The prayers of voiceless lips.
       The Wallowa,
Vale of the winding waters, nourished us
From time beyond the memory of our legends.
Our fathers unmolested there did dwell
For countless moons, the smoke of pipe and lodge
Ascending from the wigwams that received
All strangers with true welcome; and the house

Of council loved the solemn words and songs
First uttered by the Dreamers. On the plains
No buffalo was lean; from thirsty hills
The antelope each summer boldly came
To seek the coolness of the valley springs;
And from the herds our careful arrows took
What meat the families needed but no more
Than could be dried and used. The earth was kind
To man and bird and beast, providing them
With all this life requires and teaching man
The secrets and the sacredness of nature.
The waters flowed with gladness; and the valley,
Secure between her sentinels of old,
Held to her breast green robes of finery
Or slumbered through the winter long without
A dream of fear. In this, their native home,
The Chute-pa-lu lived long and well, and walked
The paths of truth and wisdom. Neither want
Nor needless sorrow nor injustice then
Was known; for Wakan Tanka's[1] law of love;
And kindness all the people cherished in
Their lives, and in their *woemahahas* they
Acknowledged His protection with the pipe
And song and autumn feast. Low covetousness
Remained the enemy that entered not
The tribe; and had greed spoken, it would have
Been banished by each brave and sachem; for
Desire to take from others found no place
Among the people proud and happy in
Possessing what good Wanka Tanka gave
The Chute-pa-lu in the beginning.
                                          Then
Came that day when strange palefaces sat

---

[1] The Great Spirit.

With us in friendly feast and understanding,
Exchanging presents with the warriors, who
Made promises unbroken till this hour.
The strangers, Clark and Lewis, kept the sign
Of brotherhood unstained by any deed:
Their voices mild, their hands were true to all
Their peaceful words; and honor led their steps
Both to and from our valley. But the moons
Brought others who with eager eyes at once
Surveyed the valley of the winding waters;
And when their rifles stronger grew, they made
Swift claim to all the plains, their cattle foul
Displacing deer and buffalo beyond
The Bear Paw mountains, and their shapeless huts
Disfiguring the primal beauty of
A land our fathers never had profaned.
By cunning fraud they sought to steal from us
Our ancient rights, encroaching farther still
Upon the soil which now no welcome gave;
Till traitor Lawyer, urged by wily tongues,
Accepted bribe, for what was never his,
From smooth commissioners whose shameless pen
Betrayed with signatures a people's trust.
Our protest to the great white Power brought
Reply that now the Chute-pa-lu could live
Nowhere in valley, hill, or woods outside
The Lapwai Reservation. In councils three,
With Howard and his staff, our ears were deaf
To threat and boast; persuasion moved us not
To sell our fathers' graves! Then Howard, faced
In anger by Too-hul-hul-soot, brave priest
And sachem, ordered us—the Chute-pa-lu—
To leave our homes in thirty days or fight,
Armed answer of the last usurpers who
Employed lies and force against our tribe.
    What followed, brothers, is recorded in
Our hearts; and if the tribe survives subjection,

Let all the future hear from truth's own tongue
How well the Chute-pa-lu made valiant stand
Above their fathers' bones against the force
That ravaged all our valley in the name
Of freedom. Hin-mah-tee-yah-lat-kekt could
No longer now restrain young White Bird when
Our cattle, held across the stream by floods,
Were butchered by the cavalry: on the banks
Of Salmon River our retreat to battle turned.
Our bows and rifles made grim protest that
Surprised the unsuspecting horsemen in
The canyon; by Clearwater's steeper cliffs,
O'ertaken there by Howard's forces, we
Repulsed the fierce attack a day and night,
Till, driven from the front by cavalry
That struck with sudden strength, we yielded up
Our camp but led our families and the stock
To safer shelter in the Bitter Root.
Peace gave us rest a while, and hope restored
Our dream of homes in wooded vales beyond
The Little Rockies; but one dawn the voice
Of death awakened us with roaring shout
And furious bullets: there the army, led
By Gibbon, for a while swept through our camp,
Unmindful that our tattered wigwams could
Not shield the sick and helpless from the fire.
  On that wild plain we rallied what was left
Of shattered courage and, supported by
The strength of desperation, hurled the lines
Of conflict to the forest; then by night
We stole in silence to the Camas prairie,
Supplied with powder which the victory
The day before had brought us. But behind,
As morning skies put on the veil of mourning,
The soldiers robbed the grave of Looking Glass
And others, scalped dead warriors they had feared
Alive, and mutilated all the old and young

With worse than savage glee,—dark deeds on which
The eyes of civilization looked with strong
Approval! Still once more the Chute-pa-lu
Faced them who hunted us like vultures that
Descend upon the wounded deer: in this
Fair valley, desperate in the memory of
A hundred wrongs, and hopeful that the chief
Of all the Sioux, old Sitting Bull, would charge
With bellowing voice and maddened horns upon
The strengthened ranks, we made such grim defence
As only homeless men can make when war
Has struck the old and feeble down and turns
Upon the few alive. Hence, brothers, to our songs
And legends of high courage add one more
Of battle, which no Chute-pa-lu will lower
His head to sing; for here, surrounded by
The forces bent on capture or destruction,
You nobly stood four days and nights with hearts
That made death shrink from your contempt and scorn.
But round us lay the wounded, sick, and dead;
Somewhere among the frozen hills, our wives
Led starving steps of children from the gloom
Of caves; White Bird had flown by night across
The northern border; then we called a truce:
We handed our tired weapons to General Miles
So that the wounded might recover and
Our scattered families might be found before
Starvation overtook them. Quietness now reigns,
The famished know again the taste of food,
And in the *woemahahas*[2] soon shall rise once more
The chant of Dreamers. Last sundown you heard
Fresh promises the strong Republic made:
And if the path of our agreement e'er
Be ambushed by the victor, yonder mountains,
That witnessed here the Chute-pa-lu's last stand,
Shall bow their heads in everlasting woe.

2. Woemahahas, festival of thanksgiving and praise

ODE TO THE EVENING STAR

The languid dusk, awaiting yon approach
   Of evening, hears the dying voice of day
In last lament that darkness must intrude
   Upon the scenes gay in the garb of May:
      Dim grows the mist afar
   Save where the sapphire torch in golden sheen
Lights western skies; and thou, resplendent Star,
   Dost usher in thy sovereign reign between
      The earth and deeper sky ere night
Commands the lesser glow of distant orbs of light.

Night brings a solemn hush, and zephyrs mild
   On dewy beds of slumber fall asleep;
Green altars, framed in honeysuckles wild
   And rose and hyacinth in valleys deep,
      With incense fill the air.
   From gloomy glen arises one refrain
Of ancient notes, half joy and half despair,
   That mocks the mortal sense of loss and gain,
      Till cold Diana feels that want
Which in each plaintive note the very oak doth haunt.

From early childhood I have known the dream
   Of Fancy's heart that keeps the soul awake
Beneath thy gleam,—what memories that seem
   Forever just beyond the path men take
      On this long quest; but now,
   As never in the cherished past, I find

A peaceful look on Sorrow's patient brow
   Surviving all the pain Hope leaves behind,
     While Reason claims this truth of old:
God giveth unto man more than the years withhold.

Would that I knew if thou acquainted art
   With longings that pursue the human race;
What other things thou knowest in thine heart
   Than endless motion, matter, time, and space,
     Which make for man a shroud.
This life on earth is but the mystic morn
Of that eternity o'er which the cloud
   Of death an instant passes: man is born
     To learn more than existence spells,—
To find, with Truth his guide, where Beauty ever dwells.

Shine on forever, symbol of the pure,
   Till man shall make of earth a better home,
Where Hope and Justice longer far endure
   Than powers that molded Egypt, Greece, and Rome.
     For when these eyes no more
   Shall watch, as now, thine ageless beams above,
The soul shall claim, on Life's eternal shore,
   The dreams and memories which faithful Love
     Has ne'er forgotten, and with tears
Shall find the gentle friendships lost in mortal years.

MERCURY ON HIS LYRE

When Druids are haunting the tanglewood deep
Where the Oreades climb up the Helicon steep,
I tell them my tales and adventures so rare
That the satyrs all listen out in the air:
    When the stars are alight
    In the dome of the night,
    Where Diana still dwells in delight,
I sing of old legends so fervent and fair
That no spirit, escaping from Nemesis, dare
    Pass on in its desperate flight;
Then hopefully stealing to zephyrs above,
My songs are revealing the wonders of Love
Which the gods, like all mortals, still seek,
    In each aeon of life,
As the joy of the humble and meek
    In the midst of Earth's primitive strife.

When the elves are asleep
  And the whippoorwills guide
    My way through the solitude still,
  When no moccasins glide
  Where the Dryads hide
    In the flowers that gladden the hill,
    I sing in the pines by the magic old mill
  And beckon the brownies outside;—
But so deep is their sleep
That they never can keep
  Their promise to wait by the gate,

Where the sheep
   And the shepherds together abide.
So I linger alone,
   Till the dawn of the day,
By the buttress of stone
   Where the brownies still play
When my strains of delight
Mark the flight of the night
   Far over the woodlands away;
Then appears the lone form of a fairy
   Who wakens each dream
   With a piercing sunbeam
   By the mystical stream,
Where Morpheus no longer may tarry.

Now the song, overflowing
   The evening, tells
Of the beautiful Naiads rowing
   On the loneliest lake in the dells;
And each measure, exultingly growing,
   Far over the Helicon swells,
Till it trembles afar by the uttermost star
   Ere it drops to the dells,
   Where it pensively dwells
O'er the flowers and bowers
And the vine-covered towers,
   And weaves a bright dream
   For the nymphs by the stream
Where no motion the surface does mar;
   And it holds it its spell
   All the nymphs of the dell,—
     A spell that is bringing
     Strange melody, swinging
     And fitfully ringing
Fantastically, faintly, and far.

But my music that rose
   To the listening skies
Must remain in repose
Till Theseus disclose
   The place whence he flies
   With Dawn through the skies;
For Apollo may claim all the fame of my lyre:
If his vengeance be kindled, my name will expire
In the merciless flame of fierce jealousy's fire.
   Hence never again,
   In hope or in pain,
Shall the notes of my lyre to the heavens aspire;
   But mournful and slow,
   Faint, languid, and low,
   All my music shall flow
In a weird and solemn refrain,
   And shall steal to the heart
   Like a wizard's strange art,—
Like the pain in the sound of the rain.

THE RESCUE OF THE ENEMY

The bitterest night of December
    Had hidden the heavens in gloom,
And winds o'er the haunted timber
    Were moaning like voices of doom,
    Like witches attending their loom.
Not a star pierced the shadows to lighten
    The blanketed regions below,
Not a lamp in the distance to brighten
    The trackless expanses of snow;
Naught but legions of terror to frighten
    With death in that region of Woe
    Every traveler lost in the snow.

But on through the darkness and danger
    And storm of the Arctic cold,
I wandered, a destitute Ranger
    More timid and fearful than bold,
In search of the sheltering palace
    Known to us mortals as Love,—
    The heavenly haven of Love
    Erected by hands from above.
For my heart had rejected the chalice,
    The symbol of peace by the Cross,
And my soul knew no way to the palace
    As I mourned my unfortunate loss
    Of possessions earthly and gross;
And I cursed him whose covetous malice

Had taken my mansion and all
My acres, and then from my hall
Had driven me out to my fall;—
Aye, I bitterly cursed him whose malice
Had wrought my sad ruin and fall!

For hours and long hours, full weary
In body and broken and bent,
I staggered still on through the dreary
Wild tempest that did not relent,
My will and my hopes nearly spent,
In my limbs a numbness that sent
To my mind a wild fear as I went
On my way through the wilderness weary,
With neither a blanket nor tent;
And oft at the billowing curtain
Of blackness above me I peered,
Till at last in my soul I was certain
My life with that blackness was seared.

Then my mind with confusion did darken,
As the storm overcame me at last:
Ah, how pleasant to lie there and harken
To the deadening roar of the blast,
To the furious rage of the blast!
I was yielding to slumber at last
And my senses were failing me fast,
When my spirit spoke out of the past,
"Come—conquer this cowardly weakness!
The palace of Love is ahead!
This tempest has given you weakness
When you need all your courage instead
To reach shelter and safety ahead!"

With an effort my senses regaining,
And resisting the gathering sleet,
I rallied my courage from waning

And my will the grim trial to meet,
And the comfort of freezing disdaining,
    I arose to my stiffened feet:
I looked with eyes that were straining,
    But no palace my vision did greet.

Then I started; for out in the distance
    Came a cry through the terrible night:
As I listened, not far in the distance—
    It arose somewhere to my right—
    A signal of desperate plight—
A desolate cry for assistance,
    Suppressed by the storm in its might—
A wail as of futile resistance
    Against the wild storm in the night.

Then feebly I searched till I found him,
    A wanderer lost in the night,
    In a snowbank half hidden from sight,
Where winter's steel fingers had bound him
    And left him to die in the night.
And I called as around him I staggered
    And bade him now cheerful to be.—
    By my lantern enabled to see,
I looked at his countenance haggard,
    And he shrank back in horror from me;
I stared at his features so haggard,
    And, lo! it was he, it was he!
    My foe who had wrested from me
    My home and had forced me to be
    A wanderer,—aye, it was he!

Now before me my enemy cowered
    As he shrinkingly lay in the snow,
While over his body I towered
    In such rage as the demons know.
Then I reached down to kill him, but waited

To hear his last piteous plea;
And he groaned, as my anger abated,
    "Oh, mercy! Have mercy on me!
    In God's name have mercy on me!
Have pity and mercy, for yonder
    Stands the palace of shelter and rest!"
And I looked, and, behold! to my wonder,
    Where the tempest arose to its crest,
    Gleamed a light in the Haven of rest!

For some moments I stood undecided,
    Now watching yon splendor so dim,
    My purpose still deadly and grim,
But my soul by two powers divided
    By Mercy's opinion and whim:
Forgot was the storm with its madness,
    Forgotten the night with its din,
In the violent night and the madness
    Of the tempest now raging within,
Where Reason and Mercy contended
    With the forces of Hatred and Sin,
Till Mercy o'er Vengeance ascended
    In peace and forgiveness within.

And then, with the care of a brother,
    I knelt at the side of my foe
    So hopeless and weak in the snow,
And calmly I told him, "My brother,
    To the palace of Love we shall go!"
And my strength could have carried another
    As I bore him across the wild snow
    Toward the palace with welcome aglow.

The bitterest night of December
    Still covered the heavens with gloom,
And the winds o'er the haunted timber
    Were howling like voices of doom,

While on through the darkness and danger
    And storm of the Arctic cold
I struggled, a stout-hearted Ranger,
    No longer fearful but bold:
For I fought with the night and the tempest
    For the life of the helpless form,
And I won from the night and the tempest
    When I carried him in from the storm
To the warmth of that glorious Palace
    Known to us mortals as Love,
Where my enemy's covetous malice
    Now changed to a brotherly love,—
    The bond of that Kingdom above.

WINDS OF WINTER

Winds of winter, o'er the ranches
    All night you wail and howl,
Sweeping by the frozen branches
    Where the lean wolves prowl;
But your dismal voices hold me
With the tales you oft have told me,
Lest forgotten dreams enfold me
    By the flickering light.

Winds of winter, long I listen
    Beside the mellow glow,
Scarce aware of stars that glisten
    Above the wastes of snow:
Though the midnight come with sorrow,
Still the hopeful heart does borrow
Gladness of a grey tomorrow
    Neither dark nor bright.

Winds of winter, through the flurry
    Of wild and fitful blast
The daring feet of Fancy hurry
    O'er pathways to the past,
Where pale reminiscence traces
Homesteads set in wooded places,
Till the dearest forms and faces
    Bless the yearning sight.

Winds of winter, still I cherish
    The memories you bring
Of a flower that did perish
    Beside life's purest spring
When the breath of that December
Blew out autumn's feeble ember;
And I cannot but remember
    Through the livelong night.

A PARTING HYMN

Sing again that tender song
    Of the fleeting past,
Sing it softly low and long;
    For 'twill be the last
Ere we part to meet no more
By this fair, enchanted shore,
Where the wavelets murmur o'er
    Notes that die too fast.

Sing again that lightest song,
    Fairest, ere I leave:
Life at last has proven wrong
    What our hearts believe;
But those golden days forget,
When our souls in silence met,
Though their beauty linger yet
    At the hour of eve.

Sing again that poignant song,
    Love's most solemn strain:
In the years shall echo long
    All the sweet refrain;
And its faintest note shall seem
But a memory of this stream,
And the past shall be a dream,—
    All except the pain.

NAME NO MORE THE DAY WE MET

Name no more the day we met
    On the ancient shore
Of romance, which pale regret
    Haunts for evermore:
On that island beauty grew
Like the rose in morning dew,
Till our souls together knew
    Joy unknown before.

Name no more the month we met,
    Blushing month of June:
Birds with songs of rapture set
    Both our hearts in tune,
And we lingered where the flowers
Blossomed in the summer showers;
But time stole those blessed hours
    From our lives too soon.

Name no more the year we met
    By the spring of youth,
Whose deep waters, flowing yet,
    Hold a poignant truth:
Though our spirits love did share,
Death our purpose would not spare;
But somewhere above we'll care
    For each other, Ruth.

I WAITED FOR YOU

I waited for you down the lane
    As the drowsy dawn awoke,
And listened to the first refrain
    Of the robins in the oak;
And though I lingered all the morn,
You sent no word but silent scorn;
And then I learned, at least in part,
The changefulness of woman's heart.

I waited for you by the bridge
    At the pensive hour of noon,
Beside the road beyond the ridge
    Where the daisies die so soon;
But you had walked another way
To town that somber summer day:
And long I pondered in regret
The way a woman could forget.

I waited for you by the spring
    As the evening shadows grew,
And heard the gentle waters sing
    Of the fairest face I knew;
But once again you failed to keep
A promise made in trust so deep:
And when the waning moon came up,
I drank of grief's most bitter cup.

I waited for you in the night
    As I dreamed of life and love,
And you came singing with delight
    Like an angel from above:
You smiled in all your loveliness
And kissed me with a fond caress,
And we our wondrous plans retold
As in the glorious days of old.

MEMORIES IN WINTER

When December melancholy
   Broods over wood and field,
And the cedar and the holly
   Alone their garlands yield,
Memory lifts a warning finger
At the notes of yonder singer
Rising where the robins linger
     Till the wild winds blow.

When the icy breath of winter
   Has chilled the pasture pond,
And the shivering rabbits enter
   The stacks of hay beyond;
Then we hear the old owl mutter,
Watch the sparrows fly and flutter,
Thinking thoughts we cannot utter
     Of other days of snow.

When the somber nights surrender
   To dreams of vanished years,
And the pensive hours are tender
   With love's remembered tears;
Long we wander in the wildwood
Where of old a mansion mild stood,
Musing on the friends of childhood
     Whom we used to know.

THE SPRING AT THE END OF THE TRAIL

We cherish the childhood adventures
    Which gray memory fondly recalls
In dreams of the Cumberland river
    And the moonbow that haunted the Falls:
We roamed all the mountains and valleys,
    The home of the deer and the quail;
But our favorite spot in the woodland
    Was a spring at the end of a trail.

The trail was a warpath the Indians
    Once followed from river to cliff
In the years when the daring Long Hunters
    Came exploring on foot and by skiff.
But later the first of the settlers
    Marked wilderness roads of their own,
Overlooking the primitive places
    Where Cherokee legends had grown.

Though the path ran deep in the shadows
    Where the sentinels towering stood,
Our youthful hearts were as valiant
    As the yeoman that hunted with Hood;
But when, on the longer excursions,
    Our endurance would falter or fail,
Thirst led us to nature's sweet nectar
    Overflowing the spring by the trail.

Still the dearest of memory's pictures
    Was the exquisite figure and face
Of a maiden as pure as an angel
    And glowing with heavenly grace,—
My classmate in school and companion
    On each jubilant Saturday hike
Up that oldest of trails that we followed
    In the springtime and autumn alike.

When she smiled, unhappiness yielded
    To the radiance of innocent charm,
And her trusting gaze would have shielded
    Her life from the darkest of harm;
If she sang, all the choirs of nature
    With rapture her lyrics would hail,
And the creatures of solitude listened
    In the woods round the spring by the trail.

On the day she was eighteen, the neighbors
    Held a party in Cumberland Grove;
And later, near sunset, we wandered
    To the grapevine swing near the cove:
And there, in the aisles of the laurel,
    She lifted her lips unto mine
In the tenderest vow of affection
    Ever offered at altar or shrine.

That autumn the hills were in mourning,
    All stunned by the crime of cold death
Who came, like a thief in the darkness,
    And stole my beloved's sweet breath!
Through the years that have never forgotten
    That day in November to hail,
Love kneels by a mound every autumn
    Near a spring at the end of a trail.

A FATHER REMEMBERS

In the summer dawn he whistled
    Tunes that made the hollow ring
Down the distant woodland shadows
    Past the pool and grapevine swing:
Some were gay with hope and laughter,
    Some more tender than the rest;
But the tune he could not whistle
    Was the one he loved the best.

By the lamp he turned the pages
    Of an album wreathed in tears,
Musing long o'er forms and faces
    That looked out from other years:
Some were fair, and some were faded
    Like the leaves on wintry tree;
But the dearest of those pictures
    Was the one he couldn't see.

For years ago his boy would often
    Tune his harp to a quaint old song;
And years ago they played together
    At the swing when days were long.
But the harp lies by some playthings
    In a vacant room upstair,
And the grapevine swing hangs empty
    In the pensive summer air.

ASLEEP ON THE HILL

Come, Jason and Jumbo; the night
    Drives dusk from the Washita wood,
Half the candles above are alight,
    And hunting the coons will be good.
But, remember, no barking, I say,
    This side of the Chickasaw Hill,
No noise till we're well on our way;
    For John is asleep on the hill.

Oh, we hunted together for years
    From here to the Buffalo Plains,
Shared in our laughter and fears,
    And divided our losses and gains;
But last winter the blizzard was strong
    That held us on Boggy's bleak shore,—
Two days and two nights were too long,
    And John went hunting no more!

Here, both of you dogs! we will wait
    By this well for a moment or two,
As we did when our comrade was late
    Or had all the milking to do:
Hang your heads in our deepest regret,
    And dream John is answering still
To our call through the evening wet,
    As he slumbers for aye on the hill.

A SONG OF THE YEARS

Tune: *Long, Long Ago*

Come to the brook while the morning is fair,
    Playmate of mine, long ago!
Linger once more by the willows so rare,
    Playmate of mine, long ago!
There is the oak where the robins would sing
Of the pure joys that to childhood did cling
When the first violets bloomed in the spring,
    Playmate of mine, long ago!

Wait by the bridge when the noonday is warm,
    Sweetheart of mine, fair and young!
Mid the full glory of nature's bright charm,
    Sweetheart of mine, where we sung!
There we held hands in one moment of bliss
As our souls joined in that rapturous kiss,
Found all the summer no blessing but this,
    Sweetheart of mine, fair and young!

Rest by the brink in the sun's fading glow
    Darling of mine, wife of mine!
As on these pale autumn eves long ago,
    Darling and still bride of mine!
Ah, still I hear your low promise to be
Mine for all time: in your eyes yet I see
Love that has bound you forever to me,
    Darling of mine, darling mine!

NOW AND ETERNITY

A hundred years from now, dear ones,
    In distant graves we'll sleep:
Our hearts with joy no more will sing
    Nor in fresh sorrow weep;
Our dreams no longer then will roam,
We'll move no more from home to home,
Nor wait beneath night's anxious dome
    For dreams we could no keep.

A thousand years from now we'll hold
    Fond pictures of each face
That round the family table smiled
    In childhood's fleeting space;
And all the words and deeds we should
Have somehow better understood
Will show our erring hearts were good
    In love's forgiving grace.

A million years from now we'll live
    With memories far more dear
Than all the prized possessions won
    In strain and strife and fear:
The times when, one and all, we gave
To one another strength to brave
The rising wind and threatening wave
    When tragedy drew near.

Somewhere beyond the sea we'll learn
    Why goodness never dies;
Why stars of faith and duty glow
    In all the endless skies:
Then fuller knowledge will allow
Our souls to see the angels bow
Before Life's throne, where even now
    God's greatest mercy lies.

THE LAST BANQUET

A Tribute to True Brotherhood

Here in the temple of golden
    Remembrance left by the years,
Sharing a while in our olden
    Fraternity's joys and tears,
We cherish this festive occasion,
    With Memory master and host,
Far from all cunning evasion,
    Free of the flattering toast.

Fancy now beckons to childhood,
    To picnics that ended too soon,
To days we hunted the wildwood,
    Trailing the fox and the coon,
Or followed where nature pointed
    To wonders in forest and stream,
When Heaven our patience anointed
    In waiting for manhood's dream.

Fifty long years have scattered
    Us far from our native vale,
Our lives by adversity battered,
    Our laurels lost in the gale;
But all these years cannot banish
    Old friends to oblivion low,
Though we by tomorrow may vanish
    When outward the sea tides flow.

Then let us, while honor rejoices
    In comradeship simple and plain,
Lift up our tremulous voices
    In old songs of gentle refrain,
Or listen once more to the magic
    Of Mozart's exquisite spell,
Till arias gentle and tragic
    In halls of eternity swell.

Here in our temple is ended
    Our longest banquet and last;
Here merciful Time has blended
    Days of the present and past:
Look on the face of each brother,
    Slowly relinquish the glove,
No longer to greet one another
    This side of the Temple above.

FOR OLD TIMES' SAKE

For old times' sake, dear, let us climb
    The cliff behind the lane,
Where still the ancient poplars shield,
    In sunshine and in rain,
The woodland flowers childhood knew
When down the path our footsteps flew
To find the clustered grapes that grew
    Beyond the autumn grain.

For old times' sake, here let us muse
    Beside the meadow stream,
Where in our youthful days we watched
    The summer waters gleam,
As on that morning when we heard
The chanting notes of every bird,
And in our souls the music stirred
    Life's most enduring dream.

For old times' sake, let's linger where
    The pale moon casts its ray
Around the homestead, standing now
    So empty, old, and gray;
There in the shadows we shall find
The lingering memories that bind
Our lives in hopes we left behind
    Somewhere along the way.

For old times' sake, when cruel death
    Shall end our earthly bond,
We'll cherish all life's joy and grief
    In retrospection fond:
Then hold me to your heart once more
And whisper one last word before
We pass through that mysterious door
    To Love's last home beyond.

SING US A SONG

Sing us a song of the years long ago,
    When melody fashioned the tune
And harmony gave to each stanza a glow
    That we felt in December and June:
A lullaby soothing young infancy's ear
    In the old family cradle asleep,
When motherly tenderness left not a fear
    In a world full of mystery deep.

Bring back the lyrics of fairies and elves
    That dwelt by the brook near the hill,
Of adventures we held and imagined ourselves
    Long Hunters that wandered at will;
Or a ballad that wakened our earliest pride,
    Far back in the years of our youth,
In those knightly ideals that forever abide
    In the mansions of honor and truth.

Bring back the songs that exalted pure love
    In the noblest affections of life,
And that sacrament, sacred in Heaven above,
    Of the vows between husband and wife;—
But never the chants which indecency hurls
    In the movie, on screen, in the page,
As blasphemy leers at mankind and unfurls
    All the banners of filth on the stage.

Sing of the sorrows and joys of the heart
    So poignant and deep that somehow
Our lives, in communion with others, have part
    In the struggles they wage even now;
In the glorious triumphs that hallow the bond
    Of the home by the goodness of God;
In faith that has led the departed beyond
    This world and the grave and the sod.

A PIONEER TO HIS WIFE

Grive not another day, dear Mildred,
    For your father's home so fine:
Sam Russell leads some fearful settlers
    Back to western Caroline.
They will reach the peaceful Yadkin
    Ere the autumn days are o'er;
Your folks will bid you joyful welcome
    At the mansion's waiting door.

I do not blame you now for leaving,
    For this frontier life is hard:
The cabin was not built for beauty,
    And the stumps still fill the yard;
The Shawnee's tomahawk is lifted,
    Swift his arrow closer flies,
And signals, smoking in the distance,
    Haunt by noon the watchful skies.

But this is home to me, dear Mildred;
    My own hands have hewed each log,
Set deep and stout the stockade timber,
    Cleared the land in sun and fog;
And here I've found both joy and sorrow,
    To this land my soul is bound,
And here our little lad is sleeping
    Underneath yon lonely mound.

But go, my love, and I'll remember,
    Not the wife who would not stay,
But the wife who blessed my cabin
    For three summers and a day;
And when the nights of early autumn
    Turn the wilderness to frost,
My heart will dream in wild Kentucky
    Of the wife and son I lost.

A LONG HUNTER'S SONG

Beyond the Cumberlands the ember
    Of dawn lights earth and sky,
From wintry dreams the forest wakens
    To hear the wild flocks' cry;
And now the crude black bears intrude
On watchful herds with manners rude,
While I move through the solitude
    Like a stealthy, noiseless spy.

In labyrinths of leafless branches
    The somber noon delays
A solemn hour of shivering silence
    Along the frozen ways;
Red foxes dream of summer's gleam,
And listen to the panther's scream
That threatens life beyond the stream
    Where the herd no longer stays.

Beyond the gloom of grey horizon
    The evening dusk departs:
Now through the forest many a shadow
    From den and thicket darts;
A moaning owl warns kindred fowl
Of winds that bring a hungry howl
From deep ravines where dangers prowl
    Till the wary roebuck starts.

Within my hidden cave, surrounded
    By countless miles of snow
That keeps my lost companion captive,
    I watch the fire burn low:
The hunter's ear will always hear
What stealthy footsteps wander near;
But, ah! this loneliness so drear
    No mortal man should know.

THE ELF AND THE FAIRY

An elf and a fairy once started
    To earth on a nebular beam,
When downward they suddenly darted
    As one falls in a horrible dream:
They saw that the two were too heavy
    For a plane of ethereal glow;
That their lives they must pay as a levy
    Wherever they landed below.

Cried the elf in the ear of the fairy
    As a satellite passed with a hiss,
"This beam cannot possibly carry
    Us both on a journey like this.
So, I pray you, jump off, like a brother,
    With the aid of your parachute light,
And float till you find you another
    Star beam for the rest of the flight."

Said the fairy with fury, "I'll never
    Leave this for another plane;
For, you see, I'm a little too clever
    To squander the time that we gain."
He glanced at the planets in motion
    Before turning again to the elf:
"In my noodle I have a strong notion
    That you might take another yourself!"

And so through the cosmical distance,
    Where angels with wonder grow mute,
They held to their course of resistance
    And continued the stubborn dispute.
There were other beams drifting around them,
    But neither consented to yield:
Some explorers from Fairyland found them,
    Both mangled and dead, in a field.

THE CAPTURE OF TIM KNOTT

Tim Knott, the brownie, hunting went
    For frogs along the river:
The sight of his small crossbow sent
    Down every spine a shiver;
For rumors of his deadly aim
    Each venture seem to follow,
And so by word of mouth his fame
    Had spread from hill to hollow.

Two weeks ago Tim Knott had slain
    Of all the frogs the proudest
That ever croaked in shine and rain
    With voice by far the loudest;
And then, in memory of the dead,
    The frogs in a grave election,
Made him their chief who wisely said
    That silence is protection.

All morn the brownie by the brink
    Searched like a shadow noiseless,
But never did he stop to think
    Why all the frogs were voiceless.
Look where he would, he found no trace
    Of them for whom he hunted,
Till, homeward turning frowning face,
    In deep disgust he grunted.

But, being tired, he paused to rest
    Beneath a shady willow;
And, finding there a peewee's nest,
    He used it for a pillow:
For weariness he could not keep
    His eyes on things before him—
With scarce a warning slumber deep
    Next moment settled o'er him.

Two hundred froggies stole around
    The unsuspecting sleeper,
And soon his hands and feet they bound
    With thongs of purple creeper.
Meanwhile from glade and marshy spot
    Rushed others to the capture,
And, croaking loudly round Tim Knott,
    They shook him in their rapture.

Tim Knott's surprise gave way to wrath
    And frantic desperation,
As all the froggies leaped the path
    In joyful celebration:
The brownie rolled—he tried to jump—
    But every time he stumbled:
Some froggies waltzed upon a stump
    And others round him tumbled.

The birds now sang in sudden glee,
    The squirrels began to chatter,
A drowsy owl looked down to see
    What was the dreadful matter;
Just out of sight upon a hill,
    A rabbit stared in wonder;
And a raccoon, pausing near a rill,
    Began to watch and ponder.

The froggies, jeering at poor Tim,
    Danced many a lively measure,
And in the injuries heaped on him
    They took the greatest pleasure:
They licked his mouth and struck his nose,
    His scrawny neck they twisted,—
With words unfit for rhyme or prose
    He valiantly resisted.

At last the victim snapped the thongs
    With one last effort frantic,
Then ended all the mirth and songs
    As the froggies fled in panic.
Tim Knott pursued the host in flight,
    Forgetting bow and arrow,
Till all had disappeared from sight
    Deep in the river narrow.

Tim Knott, the brownie, living yet
    Where densest woods surround him,
Till his last day will not forget
    The time the froggies bound him;
And when he wanders in the oak
    These many summers after,
If he but hears one distant croak,
    It sounds to him like laughter.

THE LAST FAMILY REUNION

A few more years these bodies strong
    Will weaken with the weight of years,
And goals which we have followed long
    May vanish in low mists of tears;
But faith will never question why
We falter under darkening sky,
Nor leave us if we wander by
    The buried dreams we cherish yet.

A few more months and time will bless
    A home or two with infants young
That shall adorn with gentleness
    The heritage to which we've clung:
For hope will watch with glowing face
Our motives deep to find some space
For lofty purpose and that grace
    Which saves the soul from evil debt.

A few more hours and we shall part
    And go upon our separate ways,
Strong in dear memories every heart
    Shall treasure to the end of days;
And love will guide us till we reach
The gathering on the other beach
Across the tide, where angels teach
    God's glorious freedom from regret.

TO MY CHILDREN

To Frances, Mary, Helen, and Billy

Dear children, to your heritage be true,
    Let it your inner dwelling place adorn;
Fear not your noblest visions to pursue,
    It being this for which the soul is born.
Sweet joy, that painting by calm peace
      Hung by the hand of goodness in the soul;
      Stern honesty, the guide to honor's goal;
And gentleness which gives the spirit lease
On hope above;—these cherish for their sake,
As in your hearts fresh motives soon awake.
By rugged paths of righteousness and trust
    Let us the distant hills of life ascend;
For there existence bows not in the dust,
      There love and faith and mercy never end.

THE FAREWELL

On this strange voyage o'er the mystic deep
    Our ships once sailed a distance side by side,
So near at times no tempest high could keep
    Our hearts from meeting when the fateful tide
    Beneath us drew us closer than stern pride
Would have allowed; and once, when billows steep
Broke on the prow, I thought I heard you weep
    That this unfathomed sea should be so wide;
And when the rising winds outrode the storm
    That drove the masts apart, beneath the cloud
The flashing fury showed your dauntless form
    Still standing on the deck, as pale as proud,
Your dear hands holding high a banner brave
That signaled last farewell across the wave.

TO ONE IN HEAVEN

The faithful hands of love, dear Mother mine,
    Have built a sacred temple of the years,
Wherein the candles, Truth and Goodness, shine
    Around Life's altar sanctified with tears
    Of patient Hope; and in the night of fears
And doubts I seek, within this blessed shrine,
The strength of soul that blessed your mortal days:
Lo, while calm Meditation sings and plays
Her holy hymns with yearning all her own,
    Your gentle voice, athrill with trust and peace,
Arises from the past,—that tender tone
    Still bids my spirit from all fear to cease:
Behold, the temple fills with Beauty's breath,
Who whispers, Life is stronger far than Death.

THE DREAMER

The dreamer, musing where the golden cloud
    Of inspiration shades the realm of Thought,
    Beholds a while the vision Truth has wrought
Above Life's mystery and beyond the shroud
    That veils eternity;—what men have sought,
Lo! Genius bids him claim; by Beauty's light
Brave Love anoints him with her gentle might
    For lofty ways and pure; from sky to sod
He views the endless hosts of Life and knows
    Each generation but an hour with God:
His spirit quickened by the breath that blows
    From ages dim across the conscious clod.
He utters forth, beside this mortal stream,
The coming splendor of the prophet's Dream.

THE STAGE OF LIFE

Behind the curtains on Life's crowded stage
    Brief is the time the actors may rehearse,
In moving scenes, the parts of clown and sage
    Or noble deeds which for a time disperse
    Our fears. Earth staggers, but the universe
Moves by a sovereign Power, though the rage
Of war and crime and folly stamps this age
    Of awesome wonders with the ancient curse.
For man, exploring space and claiming ground
    On distant orbs, in science wise has grown,
Yet with the heavy chains of greed is bound
    In worship to the things he calls his own:
But through the dramas one insistent voice
Bids all mankind in love and peace rejoice.

ON THE DEATH OF A FRIEND

Dear friend and comrade of that chosen band
    Which wears the royal garments of the few,
On pilgrim feet we walked this guarded Land
    Together where the stately mansion threw
        Its peaceful shade across the evening dew;
Till from our Captain came the quick command
That leads to journeys on the distant Strand,
    And you had marched away before we knew
The summons was so near. We shall not grieve,
    For memory keeps what brotherhood was ours;
And more, since you have left us, we believe
    Eternity has filmed Time's noblest hours
To show them, now and then, on Heaven's screen
When Life has led us from this mortal scene.

TO A CHEROKEE HUNTER

Will Antlers, during these dark winter days
    Spent in the hunt the Cherokees have known
    Since ancient days, a cunning you have shown
With trap and snare, outwitting all the ways
Of fowl and beast where solitude betrays
    The careless step: by Nolichucky's own
Enchanted banks amid the forest dense,
Below the trees, we've crept in silence tense
    Upon the grey wolf howling on the rim
    Of Eagle Bluff, and in the twilight dim
Surprised the wild geese honking in suspense;
And when the fire repulsed the darkness cold
Within the hut, we've watched, in legends old,
Brave Tahlonteeskee lead his warriors bold.

GHOSTS AT WOUNDED KNEE

The ghosts of ancient warriors rise to taunt
    The town of Wounded Knee; for there, around
The barricade, wait Indians grim and gaunt.
Their fathers banded in deep woods to daunt
    Bold pioneers and restless hunters found
Along the wild frontier; they stayed to haunt,
    For forty years, the stockade, hut, and mound
    On old Kentucky's dark and bloody ground.
Let justice now confirm anew their claims,
    Their cause too long forgotten by the Law!
Let righteousness fulfill at last the aims
    Declared in treaties signed with greedy awe!
Then truth and honor shall restore good will
Such as prevailed at peaceful Plymouth Hill.

TO A PHILOSOPHER

Man's efforts somehow fail, O wisest friend,
    To grant the soul its innermost desire
    When of mysterious Life we still inquire,
Is there a place where humam motives blend
Their aims for common good, and Muses lend
More inspiration than we here may know
In dreams of Athens or in autumn's glow?
Far lies the entrance to that fairest land
    Of Wisdom's kingdom, ancient as secure,
Where Man is free by royal Truth's command;
    Hence valiant Love strives ever to endure
Beguiling evil that besets both sea and land,
Till from the past we learn that, soon or late,
None but the meek shall pass the guarded gate.

INSCRIBED TO ERIC JAMES ROLLINS

One Year Old·

Dear little laddie, proudest gift of love
    That Heaven can on parenthood bestow,
    Already with young innocence you show
Those qualities of heart that stay above
    The world's low worship of ambition low,
As millions bow in Mammon's ancient grove
To gods of greed and power. Years from now,
    When joy and sorrow enter wisdom's dome,
Give first allegiance, as life's noblest vow,
    To Honor,—valiant knight that reaches home
With medals of the soul. On this vast stage,
    If lofty Truth its purpose here defines,
    Faith will exalt each motive that refines
The role God gives alike to child and sage.

TO COLONEL ELIJAH C. KIRTLEY,

Scholar and Humanitarian

Earth's ancient university of life provides
    More learning than is found in nature, book,
    And laboratory;—you have probed each nook
And corner of a realm where wisdom guides
The soul beyond that sphere in which presides
    Vain knowledge over concepts atheists shook
    At God in proud conceit. Somewhere you took
The steeper path, o'er which no pilgrim rides,
And with high purpose humbly followed truth
    Across the heights of discipline, to reach
The lofty crags of freedom, glimpsed in youth
    And won by faith no power could impeach:
Thus have you kept, in our permissive clime,
An inner strength that ever grows with time.

IN MEMORY OF MRS. MARGARET MITCHELL

*Who departed this life at the age of
one hundred and three years*

Farewell to her who now has moved beyond
    This mortal habitation, where she dwelt
In Learning's mansion, yet without the fond
    Illusions of the worldling. Here she felt
The common human ties, each earthly bond,
    And deeper sorrows of the soul that melt
All frozen anger. She bequeathed to friends
Her priceless testament, wherein Love blends
Her patient gentleness with grace and peace,
    Which all who knew her shall forever save
As proof her journey onward did not cease
    The hour Time calmly led her to the grave,
Where she, aristocrat in heart and mind,
Smiled once at Death and left him far behind.

IN MEMORY OF MRS. MARY GOSSETT

*Upon visiting the old homesite near
Dundee, Kentucky*

This crumbling cottage was her earthly home
    Amid these woods, where shadows muse in peace
As when she told us legends proud as Rome
    And pure traditions old as classic Greece.
On many a wintry night, she guided far
    Our youthful journeys into ancient times,
Until we walked beneath the Persian star
    Or saw the Babylonians carve their rhymes.
In all those gentle years, her chosen guests
    Were music, art, and learning; and beside
The throne of truth she bowed in noble quests
    Of fairer things untouched by time and tide:—
These mourning lilacs awake to hear once more
The songs she sang beside old Rough Creek's shore.

ON THE DEATH OF
SIR WINSTON CHURCHILL

His valiant role has ended on earth's stage
    In Time's long drama of the wrong and good,
And when he passed from sight, unbent by age,
    Both Life and Death at full attention stood.
    Where once he led the ranks of brotherhood
Against the onslaughts of Oppression's rage,
    Now Freedom kneels to touch the gilded wood.
Away from storied hall, past trophies won,
    Beyond the pageantry of plume and crest,
Old England back to Bladon brings her son,
    And mourning Honor lays him there at rest;
While Destiny looks far and near to find
The next strong guide and leader of mankind.

ON THE CAUSE OF PEACE

Christmas Eve, 1965

The daring plane of peace flies low tonight
    Through dismal fogs of fear and hate and greed;
The fiends of war have long opposed its flight,
    And winds of evil blow against its speed.
    Its space can carry all men in their need
To isles of justice, free from ancient blight,
In Truth's fair kingdom, as with patient might
    Its only Pilot steers with hands that bleed.
Ahead, the fierce storms shall in time abate,
    Till valiant righteousness looks up once more,
Till flash no longer lightnings of wild hate,
    And yonder Star shines on redemption's shore,—
Till, at Love's word, the sea and sky grow still,
And Faith and Hope walk o'er the earth at will.

ON MOZART'S *MAGIC FLUTE*

With golden echoes of the Magic Flute
    The halls of old Sarastro's temple ring
In stately harmony: life bows in mute
    Amazement while enchanted voices sing
    The lofty arias, till about them cling
More wisdom and more wonder than the lute
Of Orpheus gave to men,—no doubts dispute
    The joy Tamino's noble triumphs bring.
For still we hear young Mozart gently lift
    Defeated dreams above this dusty globe,
Since Genius gave him that majestic gift
    And Music clothed him in her royal robe,
When he, undaunted by the face of death,
Endowed the legend with immortal breath.

LILADORE

Beneath this lonely pine she lies in sleep
    From which she ne'er will ope her gentle eye,
And all the zephyrs round her softly weep
    And whisper how she said her last good-bye
    Out here beneath the mourning autumn sky,
Where life and death their mutual vigil keep.
Beside her precious form of virgin grace
We gaze upon that brow, that childish face,
Until it seems that somehow she can hear
    The words which yearning love now murmurs low;
That all the while she knows that we are near,
    That on yon river childhood memories flow,
Until we dream that somehow she will find
This rose within her golden hair we bind.

ROSE OF THE SOUTH

Rose of the South, to me thou art the same
    Fair flower of life's springtime long ago,
    Ere from the wintry sky of Fate the snow
Of grief had drifted round this aging frame.
In which still burns affection's gentle flame;
And by that blessed light love sees thy name
    Engraven where the years no shadows show.
    Hence memory holds dear that lovely glow
Which smiling Beauty gave each charm divine,
And dearer still that trustful soul of thine
Which gracious Heaven gave a while to mine
    In hope as sweet as either now can know;—
Thus in this dwelling thou shalt ever bloom
In glorious hues that brighten every room.

ON LOVE IN YOUTH

Name not again the blushing vows we made
    On that fair day when life for us was young,
    And breathe no more the joyful songs we sung
Beside the spring within the gentle shade:
For all the vows, like roses fair that fade,
Have lost their tender beauty in the years,
The songs but bring the same regretful tears,
And ne'er again the spring to wistful ears
    Shall murmur where the leaves above it clung.
    Yet does the heart, by hopeless longing wrung,
Turn fondly back to hear each whisper low
    And see the promise love once deftly hung
Across life's firmament; and through the glow
Arise those songs our souls shall ever know.

IF YOU NO LONGER CARE

If you no longer care, then let us leave
    Our memories of wasted years behind
These doors we gently close; and do not grieve,
    In years to come, if you should ever find
    Mistaken words and deeds of old more kind
Than once they seemed;—so let our sorrow weave
A wreath for all the dreams you now believe
    Once lived and perished only in the mind.
Yet if, amid the throngs in concert halls,
    Some pensive notes arise from other years,
Or if a voice your name still softly calls
    When loneliness bows down in futile tears,
Oh, then recall, though with the old regret,
How fair the roses bloomed the day we met.

A HUSBAND'S APOLOGY

Forgive me, Dear, if I but clasp your hand
    In breathless parting when, in livery due,
Stern death shall lead me to another land:
Forgive me then if you should understand
    This loyal heart held only love for you;
    That down the years, so often grey or blue,
These lips knew not the art of making grand
    The slightest compliment, however true.
Forgive that in pride's highest cell I kept
    Some motives worthy of your trustful gaze,
When midst new sorrows, even while you wept,
    My soul bowed down along repentant ways;—
Hence life shall keep, to cherish and refine,
Each fond remembrance yours as much as mine.

EGYPT

By earth's most ancient piles of pillared stone
    Unwary creatures crawl: the sacred mound,
    Tomb, pyramid, and sphinx now heed no sound
Across the dismal plain, but dream alone
Of pomp and splendor that adorned the throne
    Whereon proud Ramses ruled; deep underground
    Dim scrolls reflect the light that shone around
When fifty centuries were Egypt's own.
The last reign of the Ptolemies is past,
    Unknown the street which slave and Pharaoh trod,
Unmarked the place where Theban temple cast
    Despotic shadow;—Egypt lost her rod,
Her crown, her life: lo, silence was her last
    Long dynasty, and death her greatest god.

ON TACITUS

In ancient Rome, when treachery and wrong
    Sat with Domitian on that throne of blood,
    And honest homes were shaken by the flood
Of vice and crime, and horror held the throng;
Brave Tacitus, like Pliny true and strong,
Escaped the royal rage but saw the lives
Of noble neighbors fall by plotting knives.
That red reign o'er, with truth's impartial pen
    He traced the times on history's grim page,
Placed in his *Annals* pictures of the men
    Who wore the crown aright or cursed the age:
Though threatened by the beast in purple den,
With loftiness of mind and soul he stood
Where honor called him for the empire's good.

TO WILLIAM CANDLER RAYBURN

On His First Birthday

My son, see where the proud, prophetic hand
    Of expectation weaves full many a dream
Of comradeship in bright tomorrow's land
    Where, roaming in the forest by a stream,
We shall converse with nature, learn each mood
    In which she tells her secrets manifold,
    And feel the nameless mysteries of old
Which in the sylvan depths forever brood.
And when your steps more sturdy have become,
    Down ancient Indian trails we'll wander far
Where Cherokee and Choctaw made their home
    In tribal peace beneath the southern star:
There will we watch, by haunted cave and mound,
Tall phantom hunters gliding o'er the ground.

                                               April 24, 1926

ON ABRAHAM LINCOLN'S BIRTHPLACE

Hodgenville, Kentucky

Tall sentinels of Fame stand solemn guard
    Around this monument, in history sublime,
Where Freedom dwells in reverence to award
    One hallowed day with luster for all time.
    Here patriotism needs no speech, no chime,
No loud parade down street and sacred sward;
For o'er the years this lone Memorial sheds
    A radiance bright across a nation proud,
To give men courage injustice ever dreads;
    To send new vision if oppression's cloud
Should cast its evil shadow o'er the soil,
Obscuring still the worth of honest toil:
Here watchful planes, patrolling yonder sky,
Salute with valiant wings when passing by.

ON THE RECLAMATION OF ART

Written after the restoration of many of the famous masterpieces of painting and sculpture from the high waters that flooded Florence, Italy, in November, 1966

The anxious centuries have knelt in praise
    For one whole year to watch untiring love
From Arno's slimy depths with patience raise
    Art's rarest treasure to its place above
The tides of Time, that Beauty still may hold
The priceless gifts of Genius, new and old:
Proud Titian and Raphael dry their tears,
    John Baptist gazes with prophetic face
From Croce's walls, and Angelo appears
    Beside his David pure in youthful grace;
And through Ghiberti's Doors of Paradise,
    By yearnings borne beyond the sea and sod,
The souls of men from dark disaster rise
    To claim their kinship with the living God.